Misty Phoenix was born at St. Mary's hospital in Côte-des-Neiges, raised in Montréal, Québec, Canada. Now 55 years old, she is a single mother of two that struggled to provide for her children living in the hood. Her parents are from Yarmouth, Nova Scotia and she is the second youngest of six siblings.

I would like to dedicate this book to my brother Melvin Jr. for the unconditional love,
support and thoughtfulness he has given me the peacemaker of the family.

To my parents Ethel and Melvin Sr. Jarvis, I Thank God for you both everyday truly
grateful, thankful and appreciate all that you have done and continue to do.

To my children Brandon and Kateisha, we have overcome the trials, tribulations and
struggles and are stronger for it.

To my grandsons Ayden, Kai and Logan, I love you in this lifetime and all others.
To my sisters Stephanie, Myra, Maggie and Kimela amazing women I will always love.

Misty Phoenix

SERENITY

AUSTIN MACAULEY PUBLISHERS®

LONDON • CAMBRIDGE • NEW YORK • SHARJAH

Ordering Information
Quantity sales: Special discounts are available on quantity purchases by corporations, associations, and others. For details, contact the publisher at the address below.

Publisher's Cataloging-in-Publication data
Phoenix, Misty
Serenity

ISBN 9798891558212 (Paperback)
ISBN 9798891558229 (ePub e-book)

Library of Congress Control Number: 2024916227

www.austinmacauley.com/us

First Published 2024
Austin Macauley Publishers LLC
40 Wall Street, 33rd Floor, Suite 3302
New York, NY 10005
USA

mail-usa@austinmacauley.com
+1 (646) 5125767

I would like to thank God, the universe, Angels, ancestors, ascended masters and spirit guides truly grateful and thankful.

I would like to thank Austin Macauley Publishers for giving me the opportunity to surpass my wildest dreams.

Table of Contents

Hourglass

Time catches what the breath has released.
Worries doubts of yester years
Building climbing going up them stairs
Ladder of success.
I guess
Windfall peak.
Leak, seek, sneak a look at the future
Crystal ball
Fortune teller
Seller
Of great secrets kept to ourselves.

Reflection

Noise surround sound.
Coming out of their mouths
Loud like a mouse.
Circling me
Getting ready to pounce
Look inside
The mirror reflects.
The specks.
We all need to clean
Don't look at me
You will see
The image of yourself.

My Voice

I don't recognize it
It is off chorus, it is out of sync
It sounds hoarse and of course
I know it is not my voice.
I have been afraid
And
I kept it in from my kin
I know it is a sin
To hide
From the truth and not let light in.
I shout, I scream, I hide,
I lie, I avoid
I know it is not my voice
I find the calm,
I enter the Light and step through the door
I quietly say no more
To know
I finally found my voice

Self-Worth

Swing, Sweet, home
I roam looking for the buffalo
Raising, hazing, grazing the fields.
Play, level, game
I don't feel shame, no need to blame
They always said it takes two
Her soul is pure
Swing, sweet, home
She roams looking for the man
Swing, Sweet, home
That will fill and Complete
Swing, sweet, home
Strong, long, wrong
Swing, Sweet, home
She feels lost
Swing, sweet, home
But closer to winning at any cost
I'm found, not bound to accept
Anything that comes around
Town, clown, frown upon me
Swing, Sweet, home

Broken Hearted

He consumes me
When I Sleep
I dream of him
When I'm awake.
I think of him
The pain washes over me
Like water flowing in a shower
The pain washes through me
Like a bulldozer taking down a wall.
The Pain, the pain, the pain
I'm in a trance of continual,
Perpetual pain that brings me to my knees.
And oh, how I cry like a baby
Needing to nurse
Oh, how I wail and bay like
My Kindred wolves in the full
Of the Moonlight
Wanting to find my way home
Lost in the sea of emotions
Drowning in the pain, the pain, the pain
In the rain
You don't see my tears.

Letting Go

I cry my little eye
I sigh my little heart
I say bye
To the places, people, things
Stings, strings, brings
Me to the lower levels
I want to fly with the birds
I want to soar with the eagles
I want to lounge with the doves
On a river bank
In the sun
Hazy, lazy, wondrous day.

Out of the Darkness

Healing light shining bright
Shine within shine thin
Shine, shine, shine within
Blossom, bloom and grow
Orange, yellow, bright red
Let the love flow
No more darkness stop fear
Stand strong and hold dear
Let the light shine within
Shining bright lily, gentle and white
Are the wings I am given
To fly, fly, fly and shine, shine
Shine bright within.

Acceptance

Eyes so blue, so blue.
How true are you to you
Eyes so blue, so blue
How true are they to you
Eyes so blue, so blue
Try to catch up to you.
Eyes so blue, so blue
Love you
Eyes so blue, so true

Police

Run, dodge, don't look
Walk, breathe slow they don't know
Hopefully they won't stop
You never know when they will
Change their flow from go
To stop ho
They can be brutal
Or nice
Depends on the call
If made twice
A hello or door broke down
You don't want more than one
It's like an army of ants
Swarming the tree
Taking the picnic home for free
Not to Judge but that's what
My experience be.

Anxiety

LOST
Losing control
What is this frightening feeling inside of me.
Drowning tossed about at sea
What is this frightening feeling inside of me

I can't see where I need to be
What is this frightening feeling inside of me

GOD will lead
Set me free
On a path that is righteous
And
Release me from the bonds that be
That bind and tie
Fear, wear

Tear you down until you're 6 feet underground.

Twin Flame

I prayed to forget him,
I wish
I hoped
I dreamed to forget him
The only thing left to do is surrender
To the pain, the hurt, the memories,
Feel it
Remember it.
Then let it go.
It sucks when you are so connected
To another
Who doesn't want you,
Much less
Acknowledge it.
I feel him deep in my soul, my bones, my heart
Start the tears let them flow
Hoping to wash away the pain from my soul.

My Precious Heart

Detect, reflect, deflect
That was bold stole sold
My precious heart
Who minimize size of hurt
And pain
To gain fame, lame, name
Blame on me
My precious heart
Snare, dare, repair
My precious heart

One day at a time to find
The love that will heal
My precious heart
To give again not hold
In shame
My precious heart

My Mother

You are the fire of the Sun
You are the calm of the Moon
Twilight and first morning dew
You are my teacher that leads
By example with strength and grace
You face whatever challenges
Are thrown your way.
You are a beauty to be reckoned with
GOD help the man who forsakes,
Mistakes and escalates
The wrong situation
They will blunder and wonder
While you destroy them with thunder
My beautiful Queen
My friend to the end
My Mother

Oppression

It did not start this way
It was not meant to be
But, yet it is
Division, separation, oppression.
They took our kings shackled,
Whipped, hung and strung
To their men and women.
They took our queens
Stripped
Used, abused, vanished
Out of sight
Without the women
There is no life
'They have starved us, sold us and
Killed us
They just keep taking, faking and forsaking,
Differences is what makes us all beautiful'

Our History

It's a doggy dog world
Mad, Rabid, Chained
PAINED
Other men have gained
Bargained, lied, stole, killed.
Fields filled
Blood spilled
Memorials, statues, museums
Built
To honor, remember and Validate
What is the truth?
What is said, written, legislated
OR
What is hidden, denied and not
Spoken
Token
Broken

Bitch

Back stabbing
Son of a witch
Tried to drop me in a ditch
Which
I climbed out
Karma
Dharma
Life's road
Will surely hold
Something special for you
Switch, hitch, bitch
Don't want to be you.

Man

Man, oh man
Man takes
Man hates
Man lies
Man denies
Left to drift at sea
Man, oh Man
Man gives
To live
Man loves
To show
Words can open doors
Man, oh Man
We can be the best or the worst
There is no in-between
Which will it be
Can't want to see.

Feeling

I feel weak, I feel strong
I feel positive, I feel wrong
I feel fulfilled, I feel empty
I feel, I feel, I feel
Searching, wandering going along
Swaying, falling, stumbling in a fog
Follow the sun the warmth the love
Follow it home.
That road leads nowhere fast, last
Dash back because you feel alone.
Not a good reason you've left to roam
Quick follow the sun back home.

Loneliness

Silence as loud as thunder
Wishes falling like rain
Hope like the San Francisco bridge
Loneliness, like a cloak that hovers,
Covers and smothers me.
I look in the mirror while the Mirror
Looks into me.
A Reflection that's deep and wide like
The Grand Canyon
Why? Why? Why deny can you
Lie like the rug that covers the floor
As sure as you see
The Ant coming through the door
Silence as loud as thunder
I'm asking for help like a mime
I don't know which way to go
Dear LORD
Why? why? why save me
Desperation, respiration, determination

Vanity

Vain light like an elephant
Large like a mouse
What do we gain
Riches like a poor man
Striving, driving, no denying
Like none
No other
Vain let them eat cake
Draped in the finest that spiders can make
Soaked in what nourishes babies
What do we gain
Mount Sinai to the river Jordon
Let it go, let it flow
The scorpion has kissed the frog
And said good night
Vain what do we gain
Who will tuck you in tonight.

Self-Control

Self-control what does that mean to you?
Will power, dominate, subjugate
Up, down it surrounds it encompasses-
It's all of these and none of them

Ying yang good bad
We want it but few work
For it, on it, towards it.
It's in all of us

As is love, life and light
What do we do for it.
Steal, lie, beg and cheat
Look in the mirror what do you see
Self-control what does that mean to you?

The System

Government, a man-made Institution
That started out
One way and has ended up
Being another
They say Unity and then scrutinize with punity.
Chaos, violence, destruction
Is the key phrase
If you're a politician
In these days,
They call it the constitution but
They have us walking the streets
Like prostitution we bring them
The money honey,
Society still waiting for restitution
For past dirty deeds done.
Why bother who needs compensation
When illness becomes stillness,
Wrong is called right viewed in
Plain sight the selling of your
Soul for a price.

Life

Shit, love and care
That's what's brought us here
Ask me, ask me
Do I care?
Fare, stare.
The struggles flaws and faults.
Lost in the faze, haze, maze of life
Is there a button for reset
Depends
What do you see
When you look in the mirror

My Savior

You won't break me
He won't break me
They won't break me
Only GOD can break me
And he won't
So, try to break me, take me,
Snake me, forsake me.
I have him on my side
Standing in the light of dawn
Swans dancing with the angels,
Fawns prancing with the fairies
This is the light inside of me
You won't break me
Only GOD can.

Twirly Tail

I am afraid of that squirrel
It's true.
I had a tetanus shot
That's true
But I still don't want to get
Bit by you.
Squirrelly, twirly tail
Beady little eyes
Do they lie
What will you do next
If cornered or vex

Generational Cycles

My son is teaching the father
How to be a man and stand up
For what is right you do not
Need to fight be humble and
Voice your opinion and let GOD's
Dominion answer you at night

The Hard Way

I cry my soul into a bowl
That's filled and overflows
Only to
Grow and blow back
The wack, crack, black
Shit that started
The flow in the first place

My tears are silent
My heart thuds loud
And rocks my body
My cry is like a wolf
Calling home
I roam lost, wild and free
I stare bare near dare
I do know few flew
But I did, what had to be fun sun done

Green

She was always jealous of you
Was it your color,
Was it your hair
Was it because you were fair
Was it your character,
Was it your ethnicity,
Was it because you had kids for her brother

What is it about you
That makes her want to see you
Cry die a little more inside.

Unpredictable

They say the world is so unkind
Mother nature brutal
Wind unyielding
Rain pounding
Lightening striking
Thunder roaring
Man is this and more.

Compassion

She is a gentle breeze A sweet song in a cruel hard world
She has helped me in ways
She will never know and has led by example
Am I what she would like
Probably not,
But I am what she tries to love
And I can't ask for more than that!

Caged Flower

You are too beautiful, smart and bright
To let a man beat, bang. and dominate you
To take flight.
He is jealous of your light
So, he tries to destroy it
With his plight
Of evil tarnish and fear
Oh dear
I smell it from here
Steer clear
Best beware the cliff is near

Choices

It's not Rejection
Its redirection and protection
It's not selection or neglection
GOD suggest and corrects
And let us do the rest
To test
Best show our love to one another.

Condolences

The heartbreak of losing a loved one.
There are different ways but the pain always stays.
The memories help but fade as time passes by.
What do we cling to
So as never to forget, regret
We didn't keep the material it fades to
Like the memories
All that's left is we loved them
Even the love fades overtime
Like the picture you held of them inside that frame
Which is falling apart
As you felt
At the start
Of losing them.

Empathy

I've heard them say
"Why would you do that?"
From your point of view,
It doesn't make sense
Fence, pretense
Put yourself in their shoes
From their point of view, it makes perfect sense.
Dense hence
Now the reasons for doing it
Whether arrogance or ignorance out of desperation, salvation, separation, domination, isolation, fear, despair, anger, lust, frustration, irritation,
That's their choice of action fraction, traction, redaction.

Philophobia

I'm here looking at you looking at me
Wondering what could be
No need
You won't say the words
I crave, want, need to hear.
You fear the feelings, emotions, desire
That stir and light your fire
For me.

Stop please don't fear
What you hear
Your heart saying.
Give yourself to me
Let me in
There is no sin,
Trust,
Control the lust
Desire,
Kindle fire,
Flames unite.

Self-Healing

An iridescent light
Beaming, booming looming
In the distant
Sun glowing, growing, showing
Its magnificent colors.

Hues only nature could make
Take
In an instant
Breath, blink, think
How grateful I am to be alive.

Standing still on a hill
Overlooking the landscape
An echo of
Don't look past, fast, last thoughts behind.
I'm here now
In the present working on me,
She be
The gift needed to be set free.

Communication

Don't hate,
Appreciate,
Congratulate
But don't perpetrate
To regulate
Did you just regurgitate
Fate is fate?

Leave jealous alone, drone, tone
Down the green
To be seen
In the light.
Stay bright
Fight
The hatred
That is overcoming everyone
In these days
Of uncertainty.

Shadow Work

All the dark places we hide
In our minds, hearts and souls.
I want to learn to let go
How do I let go
It all flows
To places
We don't want to go.

Dark shadow of the soul
Work through it,
Feel it,
Deal it
Can't steal it
Salvation is on the other side
Why lie
Before we die
We don't want to fry
But lay in the sun.

Deceived

I gave you my love
You were looking for fame
It was only a game.

You spit in my face,
You cut my flower,
My rose is disfigured
Trying to,
Wanting to destroy,
You will never take my power.
Towering over,
You left your mark.
I was blinded by the sparks
Failed to see
You were not a man
Just a lost little boy
Looking for mommy,
Dummy
Shame on you,
Fool
I am true.

Possibility

Excite
Oh, what a night
IRRATE
Wait to hear
Good bye, good bye, good bye
The night will fly
And pass you by.
Waiting on the man
With the plan
That will fan
The flames of desire
Coursing through my body
Like a hot flash.

Sweat running down my body flushed and warm.

Dripping like sweet honey dew
Listen to the cat's meow.

My Father

You are my hero
You tolerate zero
Bad behavior
My savior
Over bad boys
You have nice toys
And things
All along you sing,
hum and dance
To a fun song

My hero.
My father

Dedicated to the Publishers

Oh, stop the might
And just say alright
Let's get this done.
Son
Let's unite
Just say yes
And you will never guess
The choice you made was right.

The abundance you will receive
Will let you know indeed
The partnership was meant to be
A trip to the outer reaches of the universe
That is blessed and destined to be.

Self-Love

I have to let go
A dream maybe
In the next lifetime
It is meant to be
I have to let you go,
I can no longer wait
On the sidelines
To see if you grow.

It is not meant to be
You and me
Has taken a long time
For me to see.
It wasn't love
It was attraction, lust and greed.
Our love was not a seed

But a physical need
I have to look at
What's wrong with me

In order to find
A good healthy love for me,
I have to look
Inside and see
My self-worth
I am
All that I need
Love yourself
Let that seed grow
For self-love will overflow.

Ayden

Ayden is my dragon

That slays,
Days,
Stays
In the same loving way
Every day,
All day
In every way.
My Grandson

See Me

Docile,
Submissive,
Dismissive
Like I'm not even there,
Wear,
Tear,
Destroy,
Annoy,
Blind,
Find
The time
See me.

Do you see me

Aggressive,
Violent,
Fight,
Night,
Light,
Might
I be seen
In between
The wants and desire
That fire and fuel
The fool
That refuses to see me
See me
I have risen above and beyond
No longer

Waiting on that wand
To wave
And magically appear
Fear,
Near,
There

Now you see me.

Boss

Floss, toss, boss
What a big ego
What and why
He feels the need
He must feel small indeed
In such a big frame.

What a shame
So arrogant and condescending
It will be his ending.

Falling off the pedestal
He perched
His SOB
On the throne
That he does not own
Listening to the drone
Of his voice

Trying to raise
A mini-me
In his image
Oh GOD
Please
Don't let him succeed
They will
Crash, burn, urn, turn
Upside down
Respect
Was all that was needed.

Lost

I feel numb,
Dumb,
Strumb,
Strumb,
Strumb
Like playing a guitar
How much can you know
Before you let go.
Seeing,
Being,
Leaning
On a foundation
Cracking,
Lacking,
Smacking,
My head
Forever
Moping,
Scoping,
Hoping
For a feeling
That may never come.
Am I numb or dumb
Strumb,
Hmmm,
Strumb
Umm,
Strumb
Neither one.

Humans

Co-ordinate,
Articulate,
Emulate
Why
When you try
To express,
Repress
And oppress
That in which you don't understand and fear.
Why do we want to,
Try to
And do?
In the name of GOD,
Religion
And Race.

He has many names
There are many religions
But there is only one race
The Human Race
Let's be good to each other.

Abuse

One is emotional,
The other physical
One leaves scars
That are visible
The other leaves the invisible

Both do damage.

Which do you choose

The one that tears you down
Or the one that wears you down

Both lead to a road of destruction
I have been there before
Whether watching you on yours
Or me on mine
It is weary
And so not divine

I know when I'm free,
Healing
And fine
Those options
Won't be mine.

Brandon and Kateisha

I have two

One I neglect
And one
I give to another

One
I have let down
Trying to save the other.

What do you do
When your heart
Is torn in two?

I hoped for the best
And I prayed to God
May you guide,
Protect
And shelter
Us in your loving arms.
I knew
I never left
Nor chose
One over the other.
I have unconditional love
That overflows
Like a river
For the two
I have
I will leave NEVER!!

Grandchildren

I am
I am
Indeed
Going to be a Nona
Of three.
They are going to rule,
Drool
And run
All over me
I am,
I am
Indeed
Going to be a Nona
Of three.
We will laugh,
Love
And run
In the sun
I am,
I am
Indeed
Going to be a Nona
Of three.
I can't wait
I have been blessed by GOD
And the universe
For my family tree
And the beautiful bundle of three.
May the story not end there
One day

I may hear
Oh, shut the front door
You're going to be a Nona
Of four.

Chemical Use

Running through our veins and brains
Images through a mirror,
Distorted personalities,
Perceptions
Illusions
Creating delusions
Of one-self.
Reasons,
Excuses
Told to nullify
And hide
The real pain inside
Government control,
Regulate
And distribute
All under the guise of acceptance
And the sheep flock to ingest it.
They say only the weak get addicted
Then why is the world so afflicted?
Some demons are easier to run
And the journey my friend is not fun.

But we all have our own cure
And that my friend is for sure.

Love

Here I go again
Pounding heart and aching soul.
Going down the same old road.
When will I learn to let go?
With age comes wisdom
I'm not young but I'm not old.
I'm just dumb that's what I'm told.
I open up
That's the start
Of a great beginning
Somehow ends
With us on bad paths
Far apart.
My heart torn apart,
Was I even a thought
As you moved on
Left on the side of the road
Waiting to be rescued
By another soul?
Excuses and reasons
We accept
To ignore
The neglect
And reflect
what we see
We choose to ignore
LORD, LORD, LORD
Why is falling in love so hard?
It is not my child
It is the breaking of the heart.

Secrets

Darkness that envelops, surrounds and overwhelms you.
You sunk deeper and deeper.
You wear fear like a cloak
You crave, desire, wish and hope for light.
Lost in the dark
Hearing the echoing of a clock
Tick, tock, tick, tock.
Time passing
Nothing lasting
As I am gasping to catch my breath.
Holding the beast inside
Feeling like I want to die
Ever hoping
One day to walk into the light
Where secrets take flight and can't fight.

Destiny

When I was young
Looking out
I didn't see
I didn't know
Looking towards my future
Going down winding roads.
Lost
Looking for direction
Going left
Going right
I gave my trust
Looking for affection
Instead
Found deception.
Always going forward
And never giving up
That's the motto
Life offers us.
Lessons learned
Mistakes made
Detours on the way
Some long forgotten
Hoping our dreams succeed
They say
"We end up where were destined to be".

The Future

I remember the past in order to feel.
I would rather cry tears
Than feel nothing at all.
Numb, lonely, sad
This is how I feel,
Is it real?
I put on an act
People see as strong,
I can't prove them wrong.
Numb, cold and dead.
Not sure I can move on.
I must stay strong
To hold on
For another day.
There is so much more
For sure
In store
That I cannot see
Oh, please GOD
Let it be.

My BFF

A bond that comes from wanting not needing.
Unconditional
Nonjudgmental
Honesty
Said with caring words.
Trust
With all your hopes, dreams, secrets and demons
Accepted with open arms
Shoulder to cry on
An ear to listen
A mouth to speak the truth,
Memories made
And shared for a lifetime
With the good, bad, ugly and beautiful
I have been blessed to have.
Such a friend
And her name is Shermine.

I was lost in the dark
She guided me through
To the light.
I was blinded by tears
She saw for me.

I was broken
She helped me.
She has been my light
When in a storm at sea.
Never in any lifetime
Could I forget she.
For the unconditional love
I have received
That I can never repay
Only hope to live
Each day
Showing,
Giving,
Caring
And loving
As my best friend does.

Son of Anarchy

Cheat,
Beat up on me
Now years gone by
I fly into the future
On another level
You and the devil
Can't reach,
Leech,
Teach
Me the lessons
Of doom,
Gloom
Soon the son will teach you
Follow him on the path
Rejoice in the light of love, happiness, and family.
An example of healing
From the inside
In order to love on the outside.
A young man I'm proud of
I call son.

Sellers of the Soul

Drugs, sex, money, fame
Lame, game
Are you playing
We all want something
Drugs, sex, money, fame
Isn't it all the same game
Drugs, sex, money, fame
Is Satan's game

All of Us

For those who have farted
(Fantastically amazing, resiliently talented, elevating, divinely).
And someone made them feel bad, its air released
We all do it, and everybody
Stanks.
(Standing tall all nations keeping strong).

www.ingramcontent.com/pod-product-compliance
Lightning Source LLC
Chambersburg PA
CBHW061355140726
47997CB00003B/1223